FATHERS

A CELEBRATION

J. GERARD SMITH

ST. MARTIN'S PRESS ≋ NEW YORK

ACKNOWLEDGMENTS

Although it started as a personal work, I never felt alone while creating *Fathers*. Many people helped and encouraged me as it became a book. To all these individuals, families, and organizations, my deepest gratitude.

I want to thank all the fathers and their babies for their extraordinary faith in the project, their spirit of adventure, their presence in the studio, and their heartfelt thoughts and words. And a special thank-you to the wives who understood the project, encouraged their husbands, and were often behind the scenes during the shooting.

Thanks to Al Zuckerman, my agent, who believed *Fathers* would be a most special book, and to Claire Zuckerman, my great editor and my great friend. I thank them especially for their constant vision and guidance. And thank you to all at Writers House for your help and support.

Special thanks go to Michael Denneny at St. Martin's Press for his wit, wisdom, and enthusiasm, and to Christina Prestia, who patiently guided me all along the way as the book was produced. Thanks, too, to Gretchen Achilles and Michelle McMillian for their artistic insights and the elegant design of *Fathers*.

My appreciation also goes to Ryan Basten, my assistant, who handled every detail of the project with intelligence and enthusiasm.

A special note of gratitude goes to everyone at Elite Color, my lab, especially Bill and Susan Jones, Richie, and my good and talented friend Harry Krause. And thanks to Sean Hoolihan and Kelly Hoolihan, who championed *Fathers* in its beginning stages and were always willing to help.

With all gratitude I want to thank one very special person, my own father, Jim Smith.

Finally, my most profound thanks go to Anne, my wife, for her patience, encouragement, and, above all, her love. And to my children, Laura, Luke, and Alison, who have made me strive to be, above all else, a good father. Along with all the babies in *Fathers,* I dedicate this book to them.

ISBN 0-312-26156-X

BOOK DESIGN BY MICHELLE MCMILLIAN

First Edition: June 2000

10 9 8 7 6 5 4 3 2 1

To the children in this book

and

to my children,

Laura, Luke, and Alison

INTRODUCTION

I AM A FATHER. Over twenty years ago, on September 12, my first daughter was born. In the next few years, my wife and I were blessed with a baby boy and another baby girl. I learned about being a father from a special man, my own dad. But I also learned on a day-by-day, trial-and-error basis with my three children. I am still learning. I think that is what being a father is all about. That is what life is all about.

Fathers started out with the birth of these three children, but I didn't know it at the time. I watched my babies grow, as all fathers do. Sometimes it seemed as if they would be in diapers, in Little League, in dance classes, or in the bathroom ("Daddy, I am getting ready for a *date*") forever.

Life moves on, and all of a sudden the little ones that you think of as your kids are taller than you, stronger than you, and certainly, they think, smarter than you. And when these kids start to leave home and sail into their futures, you look back and say, "Weren't they just babies?"

This looking back and thinking of my own family led me to create the series of photographs that became *Fathers*. This book is an expression of a special dream of mine. I set out to portray and share the beauty and joy of being a father, espe-

cially in that most wonderful of times, when the child is still just a baby. The reasons for creating such images, and this book, are many indeed. You will find them in the photos themselves and in the heartfelt words of these men, these fathers.

In a man's life, there are few things so miraculous as becoming a father. There are all the logical and biological events that lead up to making a man a father, but the miracle of it all, even in this technological age, still eludes scientific explanation.

Being a dad is a series of mysteries that flow one after another into one's life. Where does life come from? Where did this child come from? How can I meet this precious little baby's needs day after day? How can I be the best dad I can be and also get to work on Monday? Does he really look like me? Is that because we are both a little bald? Will I always be there for my baby, especially in times of need, or in those special times? Will I see him hit that home run? Will I see her walk down the aisle?

Am I rushing things a bit?

Becoming a father, especially in the beginning, seems to bring a man in touch with the powerful and the divine. This is what makes having a baby so extraordinary and so heavenly. What happens in the hospital, or on the way to the hospital, or at home, makes each new daddy Superman. For a delirious number of days, time stops! Life is perfect! There are small glimpses of this state of being in these images. Many men may seek holiness or enlightenment in their lifetimes. I think these fathers have touched upon it with their babies, who make these strong, big men gentle, compassionate, and full of grace.

The babies also make them *happy*. One of the biggest changes of fatherhood is the sudden ability to be able to say to anyone and everyone, "I am so happy!" Men often look back and realize, long afterwards, that they have left behind forever a happy period in their lives. They will say, "I really enjoyed my senior year in high school," or "I loved that car, no matter how many times it fell apart." They seem to regret that they did not know, at the time, how truly happy they were. But these dads do seem aware of their happiness. They are helplessly caught up in their baby's eyes and smiles, their baby's skin and wrinkles. That baby, and being a dad, is what they love. When these fathers say, "I am so happy!" they know it in that very moment and not months or years later. This realization, this being happy in the present, is a part of the power, the transformation of a man becoming a father.

Living with this joy and appreciating that he has his own baby to love and cherish can change a man forever. All of a sudden he is lifted out of himself. All his selfish wants are derailed. To stay in that unselfish place is a lifelong challenge and a big part of being a great dad.

Fathers is a book about great dads. Some assignments bring photographers to the heights of the Himalayas, to the depths of the seas, or to people and places around the globe. This book was created right in my own backyard, with people who are friends and neighbors. It came about thanks to dads

and their families who sense the beauty and the sacredness of being a dad. Some of these men are fathers for the first time; one for the fifth. Some of these babies are adopted. All of the men are caught up in the wonderful experience of having a baby in their lives.

I have not seen many photos of dads like these. In taking these natural photos, I was not trying to flout conventions or break new ground. What I have tried to do is photograph life at a time when it is, perhaps, as magical and as perfect as it will ever be. All of these fathers—old and young, experienced and inexperienced, the gentle fellow and the tough guy—are captured in moments of extraordinary humanness and tenderness.

The more you look at these photographs, the more you will see. You will find life re-creating itself again and again. You will see the patterns, the reappearances, the repetitions. Often, the look in the dad's eyes is in the baby's eyes as well. What is also being revealed is someone else's humanity.

When you start to think about these fathers and these babies, you start to encounter the miracle of creation and life on this great planet. It is as close as the crib in the next room, or those kids playing in the yard, or the young adult you just sent off to college. It is also, perhaps, as close as your elderly dad napping in the next room.

Can a single thought, a single image, a single statement capture what being a father means? No. But a series of images such as we have here does come close. I know this to be true. The dads know this to be true. In this collection is the wealth of what can be felt and explained, and what can be felt and never explained.

I see these photos, and I smile, for I see some of myself in all of these men. I am younger and slimmer. My hair is not gray. My lovely wife is heating a bottle. I am holding my babies. With this book it all returns to me, and moves my heart.

Our birth is but a sleep and a forgetting:

The soul that rises with us, our life's star,

Hath elsewhere its setting,

And cometh from afar:

Not in entire forgetfulness,

And not in utter nakedness,

But trailing clouds of glory do we come. . . .

—WILLIAM WORDSWORTH
Ode. Intimations of Immortality
from Recollections of Early Childhood

FATHERS

Alden, advertising executive and
musician, with Avery

I think fathers are more involved with their kids these days. I hope that neither of my boys will ever say, "Dad was not there."

I watch Avery's big old grin and see him do the little things that boys do without really knowing what is acceptable in society. And I just sit back, because in a few years he's not going to be able to get away with that.

Soon I'm going salmon fishing in Alaska, as I do every year, and I'm starting to get excited. I keep thinking, "I can't wait, I can't wait." But after the first day up there, I miss those little guys.

Everything I could say is really in the photo—the hopes and dreams of that old dad looking at his son, and the son looking out at the camera with his own hopes and dreams, not even knowing them yet.

Mike, cabinetmaker, with Taylor

The first time I saw her an overwhelming flush of feeling poured through my body, and I started crying immediately. Producing a healthy, beautiful baby brought more joy to my life than anything I could ever imagine. Having a child has made me relive my own childhood with adult eyes and see how much fun it is to read children's books and sing children's songs. I think the best moment is her waking up in the morning and her tired, lazy-eyed hugging and holding on, just kind of looking at me.

Hope is Taylor's middle name. When Elissa was pregnant, she went to a Chinese restaurant with friends. Her fortune cookie read, "You are filled with life's most precious gift, Hope." I've grown so much in my appreciation for Elissa. She works every day at having a great family scene together.

Troy, electrical engineer, with Tatyana

I'm twenty-three. Going through the pregnancy kind of helped me continue my own growth. There were things to put into perspective, things to get ready for, and things to accept. I was respectable and honest; I just had to accept the duties that come with being a father.

The thing I love most is her smile when I walk through the doorway. Or holding her at bedtime when she's half-asleep. At first she was so small that any little thing scared me. She'd sneeze in the middle of the night, and I was checking to make sure she was still breathing.

A child makes you look toward the future. There were a lot of things I didn't have. I want to make sure I give her every opportunity to have success in life, to do what she likes to do. I just hope she'll be happy.

Rick, law enforcer, with Amanda

Some people have scholastic accomplishments, and some have professional accomplishments, but this is entirely different. Just looking at Amanda and touching her head when I come home late and she's asleep makes the stress melt away. I think of Amanda as a gift that Erica gave me. Without Erica there would be no Amanda. They're kind of a package deal.

My greatest apprehension about her future probably has a lot to do with my profession. I hope I can teach her to respect other people, and to be courteous and responsive, but also to be cautious.

I hope we're able to provide for her above and beyond what she needs, and that there's nothing to hold her back, whether she wants to be a World Cup women's soccer team member, or a horseback rider, or anything else that might be a great experience for her.

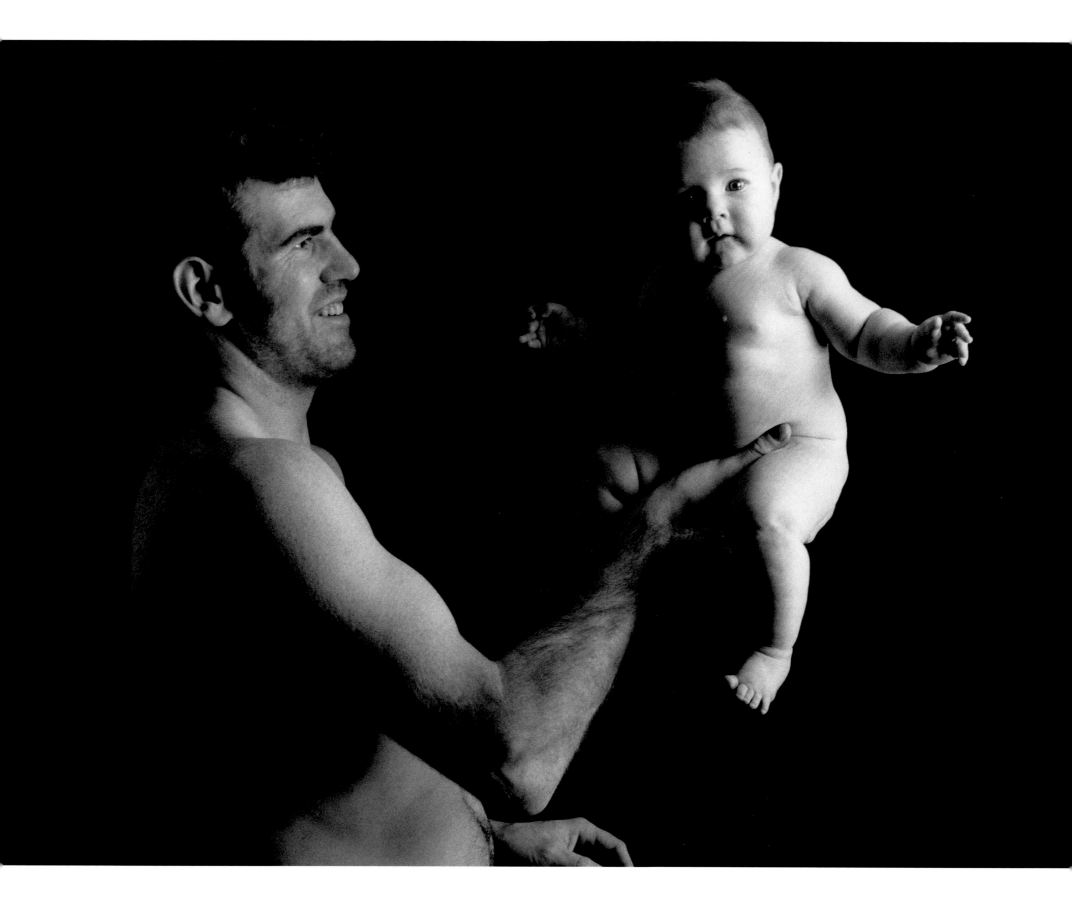

Alexander, puppeteer, with Lily

Ever since Lily was born, she's been very easy—a pure, spiritual human being. It rubbed off on me. It makes me feel calmer and more secure about being a parent.

For Susan and me, our daughters are the focus. But Susan and her ex-husband also have children together. And in both homes, we are all working for the same goal: we want them to grow up feeling loved, and protected, and smart, and as if they have a place.

I've never been afraid of dying. But now I'm afraid of dying too soon, when she's not ready. I want to see her grow up.

As long as I can remember, I wanted to be a puppeteer. I hope she will also have work she cares for, no matter what she's interested in, even if I'm not interested in it. I love to watch children love something with a passion.

Damon, hotel bellhop, with Emilia

We work split shifts. When my wife goes to work she puts Emilia in the bed with me, and I often wake up to her yelling or cooing. Having her to myself all day is nice. Recently, Christine went on vacation for the first time without her. The first night was fine. On the second day Emilia stopped eating, briefly. It got kind of interesting, trying to figure out what she wanted. I liked the feeling that I could take care of her alone if I had to.

Having the children makes us get along better. They've put our priorities straight, that's for sure. The things we used to fight about seem so petty now. The main thing I want her to experience is a lot of time with family. It's amazing how, as grandchildren, they have made my whole family happier than ever before.

Joe, teacher, with Sam

One day Sam was playing in a mound of dirt, and suddenly he had a worm in his mouth. He also ate a beetle off the coffee table. He has a penchant for bugs. I take real pleasure in simple things, like the smell of grass. But with him that pleasure is validated.

Sometimes when I hold Sam and look into his eyes, I feel I'm cradling my own ancestors. Then he cries, and I give him to his mother.

I hope he will enjoy reading, film, and the fine arts, but he might not. I want to share these things, and talk with him about them, and I don't know if it will ever happen. It doesn't matter what I want for him, though, if it's not going to make him happy—just as money will not help if he's unfulfilled in his soul.

Joe, bank loan officer, with Jordyn and Brooke

Just seeing them change and learn new tricks is amazing.

I don't think I've changed personally, but there's a new awareness now. I can't sit on the couch anymore without worrying where they are—not so much what can go wrong with them, but what they are doing when I don't see them. If you have to be someplace on time, you have to start an hour earlier; that's for sure.

Sue and I have experienced things, just having the kids around, that brought us closer together. Amazing stuff happens, and we just look at each other. "Did that just happen? Did you see the same thing I did?"

I want them to end up doing something they *want* to do, not be forced to do something just because they have to, in order to make it.

Tom, musician, with Rae Margaret

When she was born, I swear she looked up and smiled at me—just a quick smile, like "Here I am." It was a miracle, this little person sitting in the palm of my hand.

Life used to be a lot about me—my artistry and my success. But now it's about her success. She didn't ask to come into this world. We brought her here, so it's our job to be there, and to see that she has everything she needs to go for whatever she wants.

The best thing I can give her is time. For three months my wife worked, and I stayed home with the baby. It was the best thing I ever did. I wanted to experience the everydayness of taking care of her. It's an art form in itself, being able to interpret what your child needs at any moment.

Donovan, health care customer service representative, with Diamond

There's a connection that we have, when I come home. We get eye contact, and she knows "That's my dad." It's unbearable, at times. I never knew my father well, so we didn't have that connection.

I look like my father. When I played basketball at the college where he set records, the local newspaper published a story about us. I could really walk tall then. I want my daughter to have that feeling. When she does sports or academics, I want her to look out in the crowd and say, "My dad. There's my dad."

My dream is that when she gets married, I will look at her and say, "I'll give you away to him, but you're still my daughter." And we get that eye contact.

Michael, multimedia engineer, with Maya

Fatherhood grows on you. Every day has its little reward, a smile or a new noise, coming from someone who's a part of you, and who came from someone that you love, all mixed up into one little package. I always knew I wanted to have children. When I met Tara, I knew she'd be a great wife, mother, and friend. It seemed the next thing to do was have a baby.

After Maya was born, Tara was healing, and I was taking care of the baby. I took six weeks off from work. I was right there in the pits.

I love the closeness with Maya, and there's no other way to get that connection than through time spent with her. I want to be there for all the steps in her life, and there are so many: school, a boyfriend, children of her own. I just hope I don't lose communication with her.

Ken, physician, with Cora

I delivered Cora. When she came out, she was a little cone head, all pink, and she cried right away and looked great right away. I cried my eyes out. Now our big moment is when I walk in the door at night. Her whole body stiffens, and her arms flap, and she smiles and squeals as if to say, "You're home!" That's the happiest moment of my day.

Things that used to be important to me now pale in comparison. Even my own needs are second to whether she's happy and she's getting what she needs. Her being here challenges me to "get over it," to be a bigger person than I would otherwise. For instance, she gets upset when we're upset, and I see that the things we're angry about are simply not important when we have this beautiful little girl to be with.

Tom, recreational vehicle salesman, with Kyle

When I take a bath with him, he always wants to be up in my arms; he always wants to be holding on tight. And when I'm washing his hair, he's the happiest kid you could ever see.

We used to go out often with our friends. Now, to go out even one night is hard. I wouldn't say I miss it, because now my time is all taken up with Kyle and I love it. Taking care of him is our primary concern. We've discussed it, and we agree on that.

My relationship with Karen has even gotten stronger. I look at her totally differently now. We were together a long time before Kyle, and we loved each other very much. It isn't just us two anymore. We have him as the center of our life. Picking the right woman for a wife makes a big difference.

Mantee, salesman, with Mantee, Jr.

I was nervous at first, doing the pictures. He seemed more comfortable, making faces. It was a good feeling. To this day, he and I still have a closeness that people can't see, but it's there.

At night, I would get up to feed him, and three hours later she would get up. Even though it got a little stressful, I kept on with it. A lot of men think it's easy dealing with the kids, but it's work, feeding them, changing them, comforting them. It's a constant job. It's a joy as well. My dad wasn't around much. I don't ever want my kids to look at me and remember I wasn't there.

For a long time society had it that the mother should take care of the kids, and I believe fathers missed out. We love our kids just as strongly as the mothers do.

Paul, jewelry designer and manufacturer, with Andrea Giovanni

The best times are when he seems to be most alert, when I can see what causes his responses, facial movements, laughs, and gurgles. The times that hurt the most are when I see him fall over and bump his head. I see it coming, and I know it's going to be catastrophic. But he always bounces back.

He has a lot of needs, and it's staggering to realize what it takes to fulfill them. It doesn't stop; there's no pause button, no time to reflect. In our marriage, the dynamics have shifted to mother-son, father-son. There's less emphasis on our own relationship.

I will probably influence his decisions, and I'd like the impact to be positive and not to impede his natural direction. These are precious moments. This is a fleeting time. He is growing so quickly. I have to appreciate the time I have.

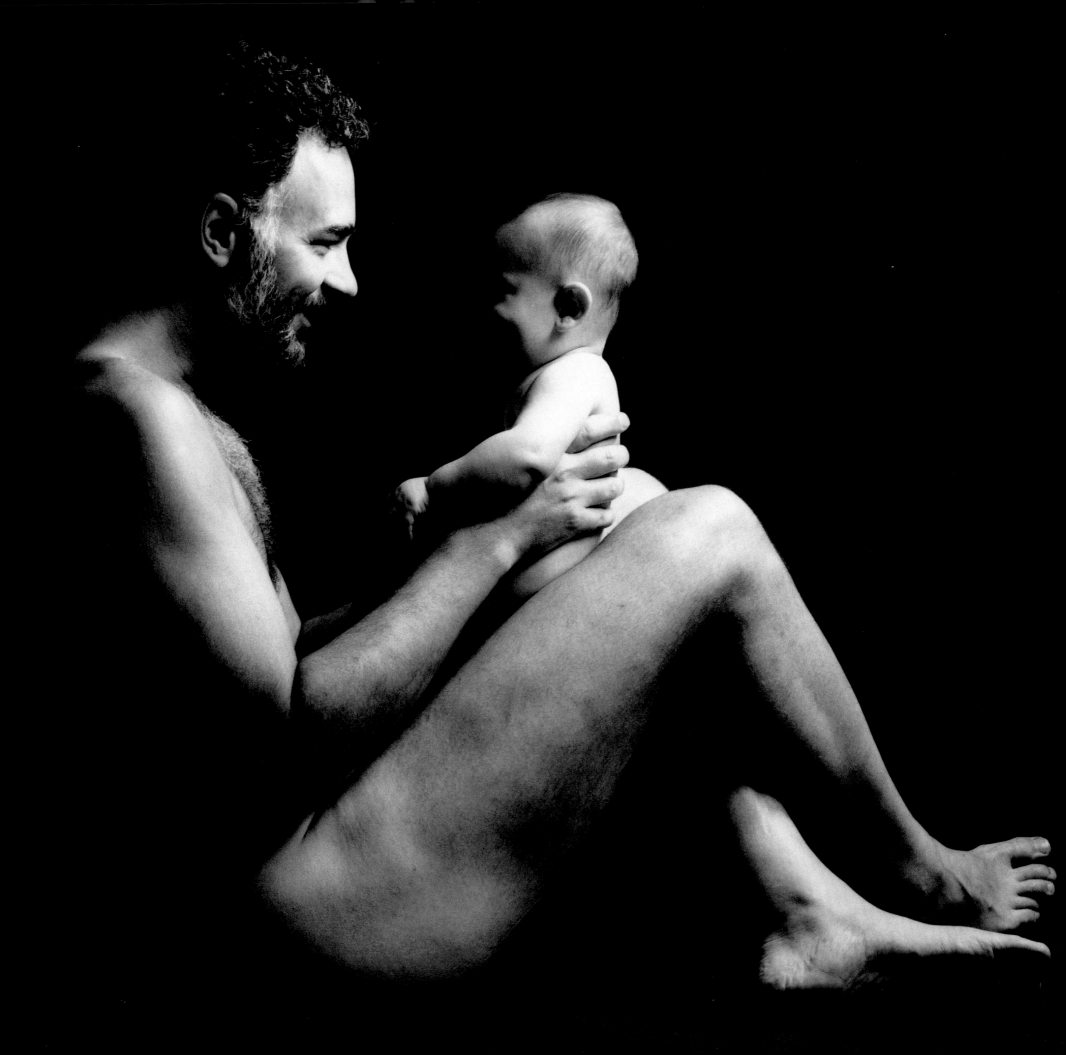

John, professional golfer, with Ethan

The absolute best part of being a father is the time when you first connect with each child. You connect in a unique way, whether it is bopping noses or doing tricks. A funny thing is that what works for the first child may not work for the second. I know that, because I have five boys.

I guess the legacy I want to leave my children is a sense of fairness, a sense of humor, and a sense of the spiritual. As I myself grew up and experienced life's turmoil, those were the things I fell back on. A child's world can be a series of moments of pure joy; a child's joy is complete. But that joy starts to fade when they begin to seek the material world, and the approval of other people. Sometimes we grownups just ruin it. For babies, a smile is a smile.

Jay, chiropractor, with Min Jee

One of the best times when I am with with Min Jee is in the pool, pulling her around in her Floatie Tube and making her laugh. She has the deepest, heartiest belly laugh I've ever heard in a little body.

My first sight of Min Jee was after she came off the plane along with two other adopted babies. She was the only one crying. Asked how she had seemed during the flight, the babies' escort said, "She's a bit of a pill." We laughed, picked her up, and saw the most beautiful baby girl.

I think a universal fear with adoptions is whether you will be able to love someone else's baby as much as your own. The minute I held her in my arms, though, I knew she was my daughter, and I loved her every bit as much as I love my other children.

Evan, musician, with Teague and Layla

My children were born at home, and seeing my beloved give birth and catching the first sight of our children in that sacred atmosphere were thrilling. My wife's strength and bravery overwhelmed me. Then I watched her blossom overnight into the most natural and confident mother. It was a revelation.

I love walking them to sleep outside, no matter what the weather. To hold the babies close in my arms, with the sights and sounds of night around us, and to feel them slowly drift off, so peaceful and secure, are a great gift.

I'm proud of the way I've handled myself as a father, a role I'd been scared to take on, although I know that no matter how much I love them, I cannot give them any guarantees in life but must trust them to powers far greater than mine.

Kurt, warehouse associate, with Alexandria

She follows her brother everywhere. Everything he does, she does. Before she was born, he didn't want her. Then he saw her in the hospital, and he figured out, "She's not going to affect me. She can't do anything." Now it's changed, of course.

Pam and I just sit there and watch them. Alex smelling a flower is hilarious. Instead of sniffing, she blows. She's always carrying one of the kittens around. If she sees a bird, she starts jumping, her little feet going. "Birdie, birdie, birdie!"

When you have kids, sometimes you lose track of each other. But then you're lying next to each other in bed, talking about the things they did that day that made you laugh, or frustrated you. They definitely complete things. I don't think of it as change. They've just made everything better. It's nice having four of us in the house.

Marko, artist, with Ihor

There's nourishment in being needed. Seeing the baby's eyes light up and knowing that he counts on me. My wife used to tell me, when she was pregnant, "You know, this baby's going to respect you. He's going to look up to you." And he already does. Nothing else in the world has done what he's done for me. He's given me a lot of pride. I've been knocked down a dozen times and brushed myself off, but this time I feel that I'm getting up on a permanent level.

He really brings out some very deep emotions. I get real heavy, and I can't help it. I look at him, and I sigh, over and over. I'm passionate about my paintings, and my friends, and my memories, but this is as intense as it gets. There's no painting in the world that tops this.

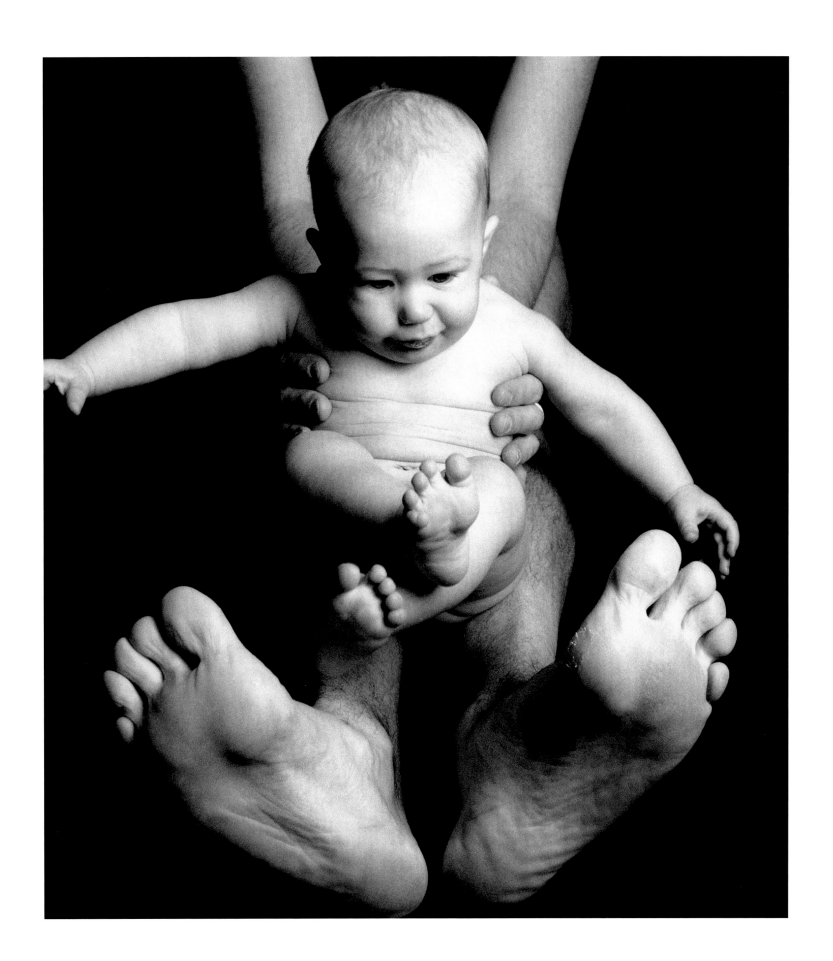

Jonathan, physician, with Isaac

On the night Isaac was born, I held him for a long time while my wife rested. During the first few days, we adapted to his rhythms of sleep and waking. Maybe it was fatigue, but our relationship took on a new, accepting calm. And, of course, we shared the inevitable concern that Isaac should always be safe. That, too, is a bond between parents.

Long before he actually smiled, his little face was an emblem of laughter in my mind. "Isaac" means "laughter" in Hebrew, so the suggestion was powerful. I saw his face, heard his wordless voice, and sensed his presence even when I was not with him. It was like falling in love all over again.

His happy disposition feels like a gift. I hope he always has rich relationships in which he can share it, an enormous curiosity about the world, and a truly felt respect for others.

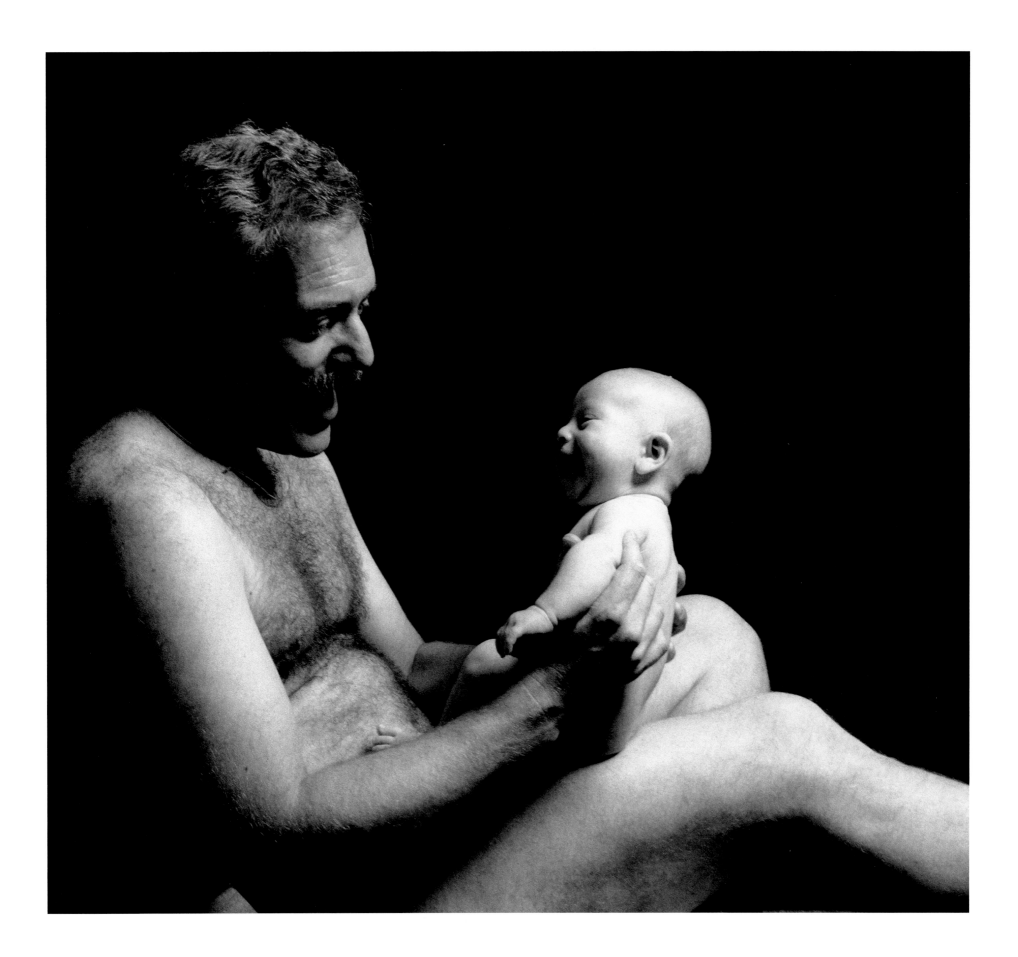

Paul, college campus maintenance supervisor, with Andrew

Andrew is a ball of joy. All I want to do is cuddle with him. I don't need to go out with the guys; I'd rather be home. I don't need to go watch a game; I'd rather play with the children. I had the glamour job at Sotheby's, doing antique shows, but now I can't imagine doing anything except what I am doing, because it allows me the freedom to be at home. I don't mind changing diapers.

My father was affectionate with me. I think that's why it comes so easy for me with Andrew. When things get hard, I try to remember how it was when I was young, and to do as my father would have done.

Susan purchased this wonderfully large couch, where we can all sit and be close together. I don't know where or what I'd be without my wife and children.

David, corrections officer, with Devon

The unconditional love that you receive from a kid is the best. I can be in a terrible mood, but when she looks at me and says, "Daddy," suddenly everything's all better.

I'm a firm believer in the old-fashioned family values—the "yes sir, no sir; yes ma'am, no ma'am" kind of thing. Sometimes I catch myself saying, "Holy Mackerel, I sound just like my father!"

I hope my daughter will be educated enough, and happy enough in herself, so she can do her own thing and be with someone she really, really wants to be with—not someone she feels she has to be with. For myself, I'd like to be around long enough to see Devon have her own children. Maybe I'll be able to spoil them a little bit more than I am able to spoil her. That would be great.

Clark, high-school administrator, with Clark L.

When I come home from work, I hope Clark will be awake so I can pick her up. She looks a little bit like me. She wants to stand up, she wants to walk, she wants to eat food, she wants to be bigger than she is.

My wife Lisa and I are both educators, so we really want her to value her education. I hope we're not too pushy. I'm already concerned about her elementary-school experience: the physical setting, the number of kids in the classroom. My world is starting to revolve around her, and as her world expands, mine will expand around hers.

I want her to be a happy person and to find her way in the world, regardless of what she wants to do with her life. I just hope it makes her happy and is safe for her.

Bob, physician, with Freeman

Since birth, he's marveled at the simplest things. It's wonderful to see that, wonderful to be part of it. It's renewing.

Having the kids has made my wife and me more separate in a lot of ways because parenting is difficult, and you're not going to agree. Yet you suddenly have this shared responsibility, too.

Being a father has made me become a little bit more mature, less reactive—and not just with him. I temper many of the things I do out of a sense that now there's a greater purpose. For example, we just bought a new vehicle. Not my idea of a great car or a fun drive, but it's what we have to do now.

I hope he can always find that laugh. I don't care what he does. I just want him to enjoy it.

Ian, actor, with Nadya

The first time I saw her it took my breath away. Instantaneously, every-thing changed. Watching my wife be pregnant all those months was hard, and then when Nadya came out and everything was fine, it almost knocked me on the floor.

Every morning, when all three of us wake up together, I say, "Good morning, Dolly," and she smiles. It's the best thing that could happen to a person.

It's frightening, sometimes, to realize that whatever I do from now on will affect her, and that I have to be completely responsible at all times about my attitude, my business life, and how I speak to her.

I hope that she doesn't have to be hurt in order to realize what true happiness is—that it comes to her a little easier than it did to me. I hope she can be comfortable with herself.

Charlie, fireman, with Josh

One of the best things about being his father is knowing there's so much of me in him and that I'll have the chance to groom him. My son is going to brush his teeth and get an education!

Nobody has a perfect life. The Lord put us here, and whether you believe in Him or not, this is still a wonderful thing, life. There's nothing in this world you can't go get yourself, period. I remember very vividly when my dad told me, "Charlie, you can do anything you want in life. Anything you want." That's all he had to tell me. I was twelve or thirteen then, and I've lived with that confidence ever since. That allows me to go through life, happy, just enjoying it. I'm going to make sure, when Josh gets to the point where he understands, to let him know the same thing.

Fred, high-school principal in a state prison, with Adrian

The best thing about being a dad is the love, the love going both ways. The smiles, the hugs, the kisses, and the tickles. God, it's so fulfilling. Walking into a room and just seeing the smiles. Loving your children. The giving and taking of love.

I never knew I could give so much. My life used to be so closed, so structured. I had things my way. My world was my work. Now, with Marcy and the kids, my world has expanded so much. I just didn't think I had it in me.

I hope my children grow up in a safe, secure, contented environment. I think that everything else will flow from that. They'll make good decisions because they're complete inside.

Rich, contractor, with Katie

It's a thrill waking up in the morning and seeing her sleeping in her crib, and just wondering what she's dreaming about. She's just a bundle of joy. I say, "Who's the most beautiful baby in the world?" There aren't enough words to say how I really feel; I just love her, dearly.

Sometimes I wake up in the middle of the night and wonder if she's breathing. The house is air-conditioned. Is she covered?

When my other kids were little, I couldn't be there for them all the time. With Katie, I have been there from the pregnancy and the day of birth, and seven months since. And it's great. I love it, I really do. It brings tears to my eyes. I love all my kids, but this is just something that I never enjoyed before.

I always tell her, "You're my bestest."

Peter, businessman, with Kayla

I am no longer the selfish guy I was. Five years ago I would not even have been able to comprehend the feeling of fatherhood. Now, I go away for a week or two at a time, and when I come home, she's doing something completely new. And her hair has grown a little bit.

The first time she and I were alone, I was holding her in my arms in the kitchen. I looked down at her, and she was looking so deeply into my eyes, as if she knew who I was and she was just checking me out. I started to cry.

I'm going to offer her the most I can, so that she'll be able to stand on her own two feet, and not be dependent on some guy.

Shawn, law enforcer, with Tim

Since Timmy arrived, I've found many more emotions in myself than I ever knew I had. I used to keep all my feelings in check. Now I notice it's a lot harder to sit through a sentimental movie and not shed a tear, especially if the movie has something to do with a child.

For the first few seconds after the birth, you're just making sure that the kid's all right. Then you realize, "Wow, that's my baby." Then, once you get over being tired, you realize how special it is to have a child. It's as if you are in your own little world now, which people without children don't understand.

There are so many people today who seem to be lost. If Timmy finds what he wants to do, and does it with his heart and soul, I will be satisfied with that accomplishment.

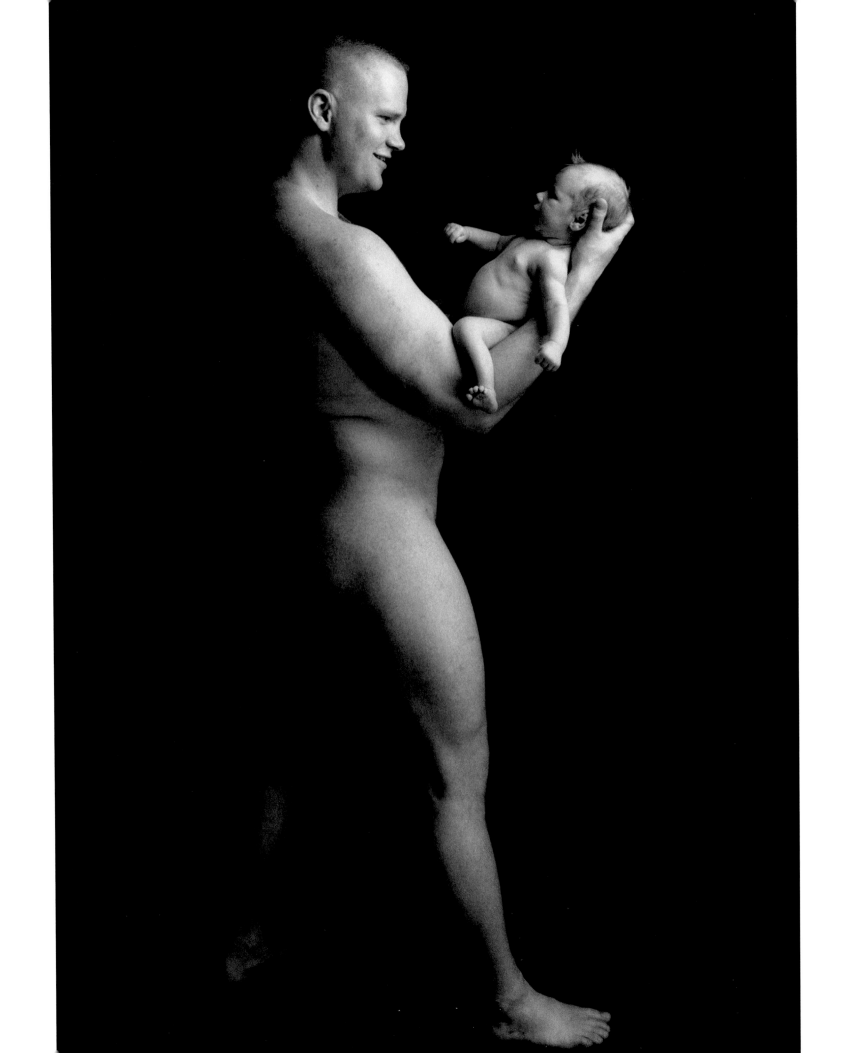

Anton, software engineer, with Sabina

My mother used to say there was nothing like the feeling of my forehead in the nape of her neck, and now I see what she meant. When a baby gives a hug back, there's nothing like it.

We don't use words so much as facial expressions and silliness. I love it, and I know *she* likes it, because when she wants my attention, she just gets goofy.

I understood before she came that we could forget going out like we used to. But once the baby came, I didn't *want* to go out. I didn't want to be away from the baby. All I could think about was the baby.

I don't want to extinguish the spark of childhood, even a little. I want her to have a sense of possibility and hope—and the ability to experience joy no matter what her circumstances may be.

Brad, actuary, with Philip

One of my favorite times with Philip is bedtime. After he's all changed, we sit in a rocking chair. He puts his head on my shoulder and hums. What goes through my heart then is fantastic. I realize that I love someone so much it has become a part of who I am. At birth, when he first appeared, and then cried, and everything was moving, I just felt so thankful—more than I could have imagined. I would have given up everything to have that moment.

My biggest hope for him is that he will be very happy. I would love it if he became a UConn basketball star. I would be thrilled if he ended up owning a company or becoming a millionaire, but the most important thing is that he'll have a big smile on his face when he's thirty years old, and be happy.

Greg, actor, with Zane Raven

What makes me happiest is coming home after being out all day and seeing the little jig he does with his feet. That really socks it to me that I'm his father. You don't have that relationship with anyone else. When he first came into the world, I saw my own father, like a hallucination—the big cycle of life.

We didn't plan the baby. The beauty is that it did happen, and how we embraced it. And by embracing the reality of having a child, we have both honestly faced each other. It's as if we said, "OK. This is what we're going to do, and we're going to do it the best we can."

I want him to be fully alive, and to appreciate the preciousness of life. For we do fade away, and we don't always recognize how sacred and how special life is.

Peter, electrician, with Forrest

No matter where I am emotionally, when I'm uptight, I'm unhappy, I'm stuck, he can look at me, and in a moment I'm transformed. That did not happen to me before there was Forrest. Being a parent is unlike any other experience of love I've known. Other love, especially romantic love, can be so, oh, *heady*. But the way I feel about Forrest is beyond words.

Sometimes I think, "What if something bad happens?" And something bad *is* going to happen to him. At some point he's going to skin his knee. And the thought of that almost makes me think, "Oh, God, why did we have to go and have him?" I want him to be out in the world, living his life richly, but my heart breaks at the thought of his heart breaking.

William, jeweler, with Benjamin

The first time I looked into Benny's eyes, I got the feeling that this little being was saying, "OK, now it's you and me. You're going to take care of me." I never thought I'd have a child, but it's the best thing I ever did, and the most profound.

Sometimes in the morning it's just the two of us having breakfast, or reading a book. I get all the attention, and that's very special because he really is a mama's boy at this age. The best times are when he says, "I really like you." I like the responsibility, too. Even though it's a little daunting, I like the way he watches what I do, and imitates me.

He's such an innocent, and he's so vulnerable. It's going to be very difficult to see him get hurt, and begin to harden, and start protecting himself. But I know it's inevitable.

Tom, law enforcement officer,
with Christopher

I love the joy in his face when I hold him, and his pleasant disposition and great sense of humor. I'm very proud to be a father. I have a good relationship with my father, and I will use that as a guide.

I was there for both my sons' births. One minute there are two of you, and the next minute there are three of you—and now four of us. I still don't believe it. Here is a little tiny being who's looking to us for everything; he just wants to know, "OK. What do you want next? What *is* next?"

I hope I'm around for the milestones in his life, and that I'll do a good job and teach him how to be a responsible and caring person. More important, I hope he won't be rushed out of his childhood, so that he can enjoy it.

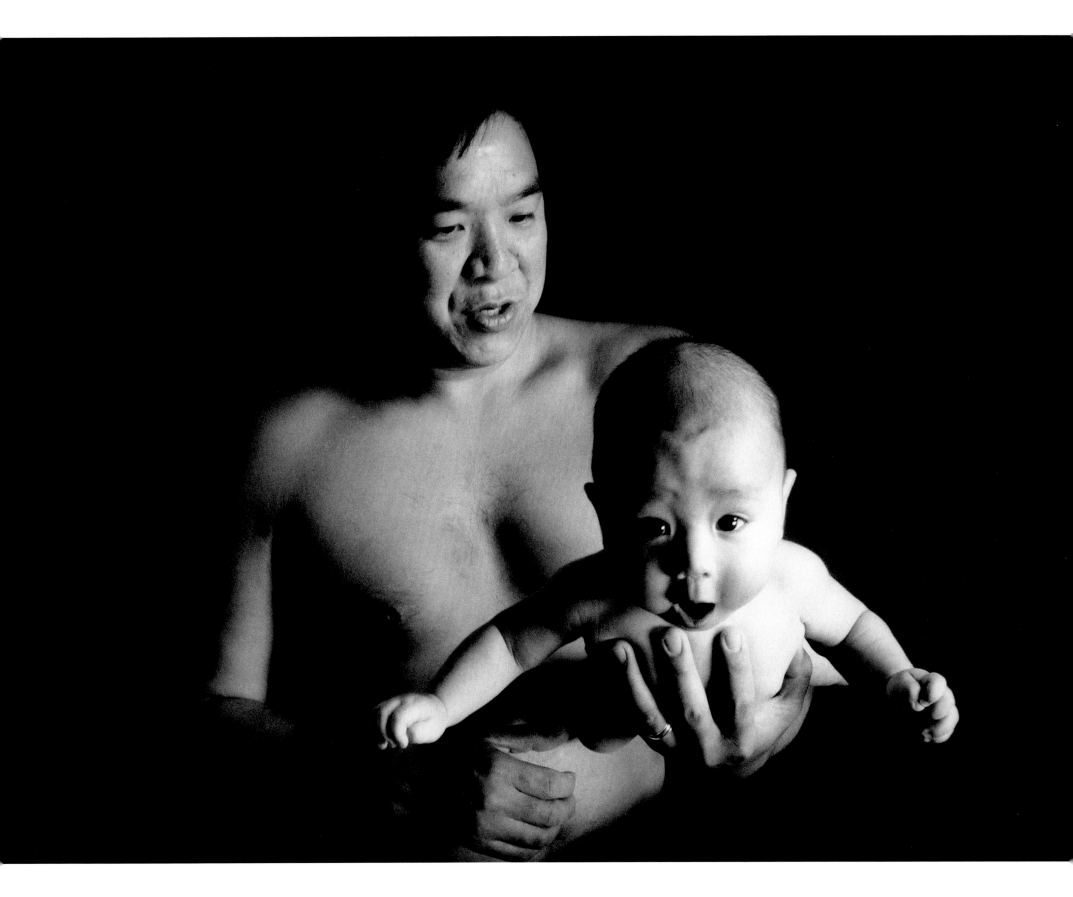

Mike, artist, with Lucy, Abbey, and Ivan

I like the physical part, when I'm spread out all over the floor and the kids are climbing all over me like monkeys.

After the sonogram, they said, "Oh, don't you know? You're having twins." We cracked up. I knew they would be girls; I only had girls' names picked out. Ivan was born at home on the floor, accidentally. He came like a fish. I look at my kids, and I think that no matter what I do as an artist, they are my greatest creation—*our* greatest creation, 'cause I didn't do it alone.

Eventually the insulated cocoon I created for my family will yield to outside influences, and TV, and people, and I'll realize that it's out of my hands. There's a lot of uncertainty out there, and a lot of danger-ous situations. Hopefully they'll have guardian angels like I did.

Lincoln, physicist, with Kiran

I see being a father as providing a service, conveying the most important lessons I've learned. Right now he's too young to talk, so I'm limited to providing a place for him to play and feel comfortable.

We go out into the woods and just sit down. He gets involved with the forest floor. Sometimes I put him in the backpack, and we go to the reservoir for a picnic supper. In the Spring I just carried him around under my coat. He's gotten too big for that now, so he goes in a jogging stroller.

I'm a late-night person, and my wife is an early-morning person, and this kid sleeps so little that he goes to bed with me and wakes up with her. He's got so much more energy, he makes us feel like old, shaggy, treelike beings, with him running around like a squirrel.

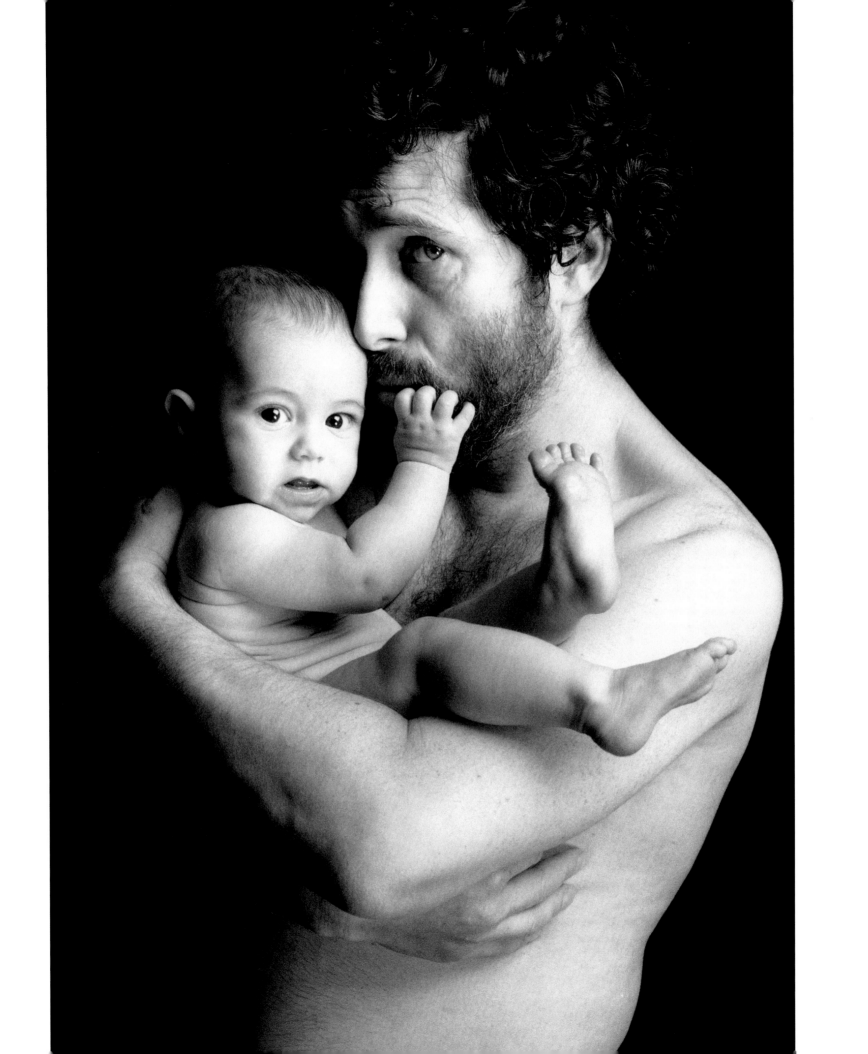

Ted, software consulting company executive, with Amanda

Amanda likes to play hard to get. I always want to hold her close and kiss her, but she pushes me away most of the time. Sometimes, though, she will let me hug her, and she hugs me back and laughs. This exchange is heavenly.

My deep love for Amanda is in some ways related to my deep love for my wife, but I also realize that my growing love for my wife is, in many ways, related to how much she loves our child.

I used to want to mold my children's lives into what I wanted for myself. As I mature, I realize that I am mostly their servant or, at best, their consultant, not the designer of their future. I hope Amanda will discover an interest that she truly loves and can pursue with her body, mind, and soul.

Rich, aviation specialist, with Kayla

She loves to play peekaboo. Sometimes she smiles at me when she wants something, and she's a heartbreaker. She always has a twinkle in her eye. During her birth, I prayed she would be a girl. We had twin boys already, and my wife really wanted to have a girl. So I was happy.

I learned a lot from my dad, especially values and responsibility. I grew up with my grandmother a little bit, too. My family was always there for me, and still is.

My wife and I are closer now. We have our ups and downs sometimes, but the kids basically keep us in line. It takes a lot, being a father. You've got to be a patient man. But you wake up every morning, and there's all the joy of seeing them.

Kirk, school custodian, with Aja

It's amazing how important she is to me. I'd jump off a cliff for her without hesitating. I love my wife, and I'd do anything for her, but I'd walk through fire in a second, without blinking, if I heard Aja crying.

At her birth, there were some anxious moments. Then she was here, and she was fine. For that one minute, everything was OK—the baby, Mom, my son at home. I didn't have to worry about anything. I was just happy, and so worn-out.

After my son was born, I told a friend I couldn't wait until I could start sleeping again. And the friend said, "Oh, you'll *never* sleep again." So far he's been right. It's been six years, and I've never again slept eight hours solid. When we leave the kids with a baby-sitter, everyone's crying, and we feel awful—because we're going to a movie.

David, engineer, with David, Jr.

Cuddling him, looking at him, and just appreciating him are the best. He's so beautiful. I wake up mornings and realize that I've missed him. I'll go over to the bassinet, and there he'll be, looking around.

It touches me how much he needs us; we're all that he has. He's so innocent. We just have to watch out for him—more than we've watched out for ourselves.

At his birth, I was scared for my wife. Whenever she has to go through any pain, I wish it could be me. So he comes out, they cut the cord, they wash him down, and they wrap him up and give him to me. He's so tiny, and Kelly's still recovering. So there's my first big decision—do I go to my wife or my son? So I sit next to her, and I hold the baby and talk to her about him.

Len, shoe store owner, with Emma

Emma and I have our private time in the morning, one on one with no distractions. And I can't think of another place I'd rather be.

My wife wanted to have a baby. I was ambivalent; it would be fine with me, but I could enjoy life as we were. I'm fifty-five, and up to now my life has been focused on what I wanted. Now Emma is the center of my universe. Getting up at six in the morning is challenging, but I'm always so blissed-out around her that I don't mind.

My daughter has been loved and hugged more in her first year than I was in my whole childhood. They used to say that if you gave your kids everything they wanted, they would become dependent on you. The reality is that they will feel safer in the world and more independent.

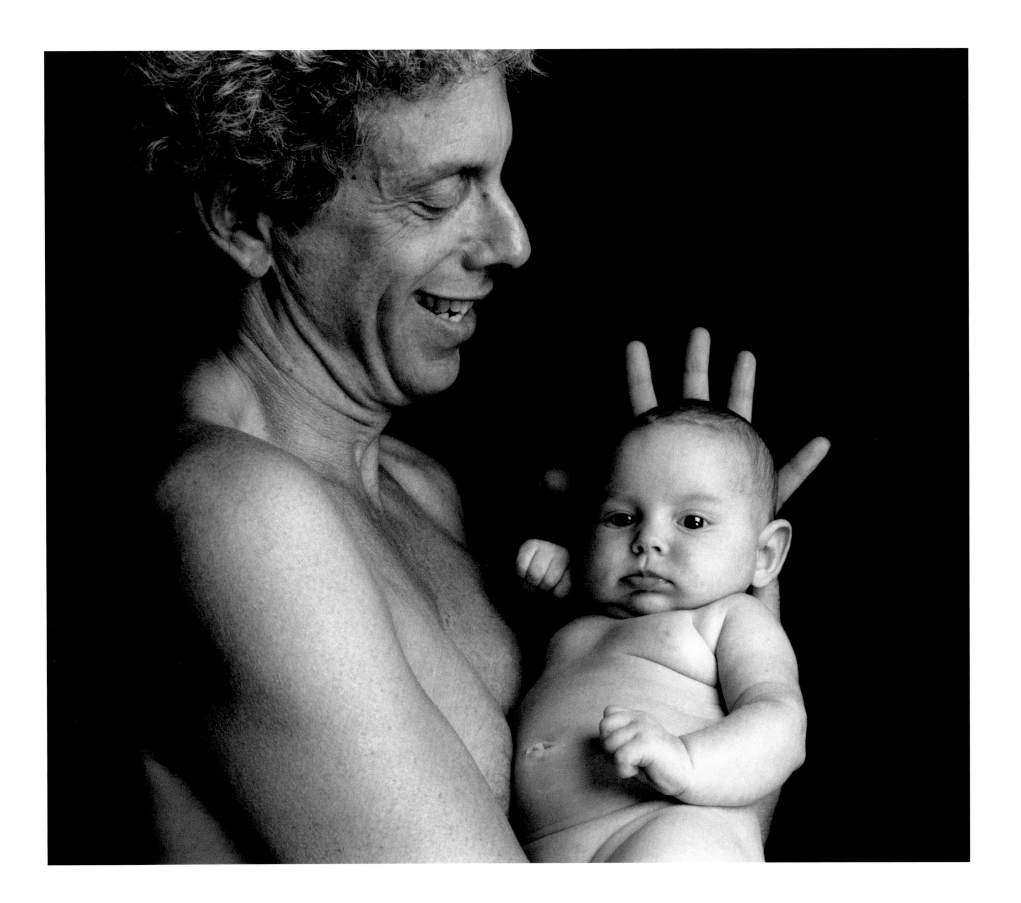

Mike, manufacturer, with Ben

I want to love and protect and nurture this little person. I fell in love with him the first day I met him, but I think that that's how it works. None of my friends who are fathers feel any differently. It went from nothing to "Here's this person I would walk in front of a truck for."

When he was born, there were a lot of births going on, and once they were OK with his breathing and everything, they said, "Here. Take him." For three to four hours Barbara and I just lay in bed, with him on our chests. We fell in love right there and then. He was very wide-eyed. I know he couldn't really focus on anything, but in some sense, I felt, he knew what was going on. Barbara and I have done lots of other things together, but this most momentous thing was ours and ours alone.

Jeff, Pepsi-Cola driver-salesman,
with Shoshana

The best thing is that her love is unconditional. No matter what kind of trouble I have during the day, I always come home to a warm, glowing hug and kiss. Everything about a baby is a joy. Every day is different. I actually delivered Shoshana. The doctor allowed me to pull her out. We didn't know she would be a girl; we didn't want to know.

I don't want her to work at a dead-end job; I want her to be at her full potential. Yet I also worry that I might push her too much.

Single friends don't understand why it's difficult for me to find time to do the things I used to do. It's a whole different mind-set; yet it just comes naturally.

Every time my wife and I look at her, it's something we can hug over, and we say, "Wow, we made this beautiful child!"

Tim, state law enforcement officer, with Nathaniel

Seeing him is like seeing a little part of myself. He's growing like me. I smile, he smiles. I can see the love from him to his mom and him to me. I maintain the discipline to try to do things that are right in my life, so that he has someone to look up to and follow.

As a father you always have to be there. You can't let your child down, not even once. If you let him down once, then you have to work on recovering from that letdown. You're going to make mistakes, and you're going to let him down, of course, but you have to keep it in your head, I think, *not* to let him down.

Carl, musician, with Ava

Since she arrived, I laugh more than I have in twenty years. The real fun at this stage of her life is eating. She ends up covered from head to toe, laughing. We also do crawling races around the house: we're both down on our hands and knees. She looks over at me and gets this devilish little smile, and tries to speed away. She's just psyched that I'm down on the floor with her.

I actually feel more grounded and stronger than before. My focus is on my family. I work all the time, and I'm happy to be doing it, because of this opportunity to make a home for her.

My biggest hope for her is that she will feel good about herself. If she can mature as she grows and have a really good sense of self, she can do whatever she wants. Everything else stems from that.

William, producer and entertainer, with Iwan and Shafi

One of the nice things about being a dad is the chance to discover things about yourself. People say you have to define who you are. Well, that is easy to do when you have not one but two duplicate models of yourself.

My dad was in my life when I was growing up. He didn't say much, but he always had a grin on his face. I used to think of him as goofy, but now I get it: sometimes all you can offer kids is a smile.

In a clinic, I saw this new father. He looked about eighteen and seemed to be uncomfortable handling the baby. I walked up to him and said, really quietly, "Hand me that baby. You hold him like this. The baby is waiting for you to tune in to him, and nobody can hold your baby better than you." The baby stopped crying. The guy said, "Thanks."

Dan, financial analyst, with Jessica

The best thing about being Jessie's father is the smile on her face when I come home, and the emotional connection. I might be absorbed in a project like painting, with five buckets of paint open. I'll put the brush down to go over and seize the moment when she needs me. Because I know that someday she won't need me.

A big fear is the specter that she might not be happy in life, that she won't be able to find herself and will take it to heart, and start withdrawing. The songwriter and artist Jewel says in one of her songs, "Something you need to know is you're all OK." And I hope that Jessie can realize that she is OK, and that whatever she decides to do in life is OK, as long as it's OK with her.